My Rhyme Time

Incy Wincy Spider

and other playing rhymes

Miles Kelly

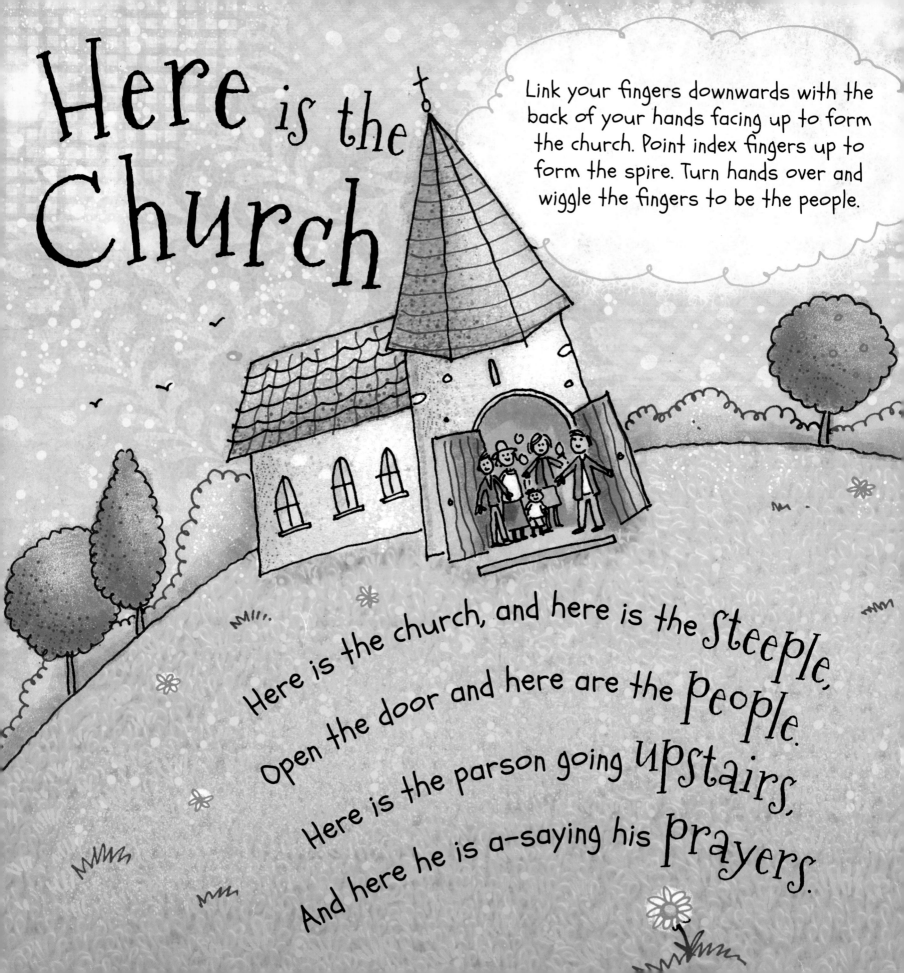

Here is the Church

Link your fingers downwards with the back of your hands facing up to form the church. Point index fingers up to form the spire. Turn hands over and wiggle the fingers to be the people.

Here is the church, and here is the steeple,
Open the door and here are the people.
Here is the parson going upstairs,
And here he is a-saying his prayers.

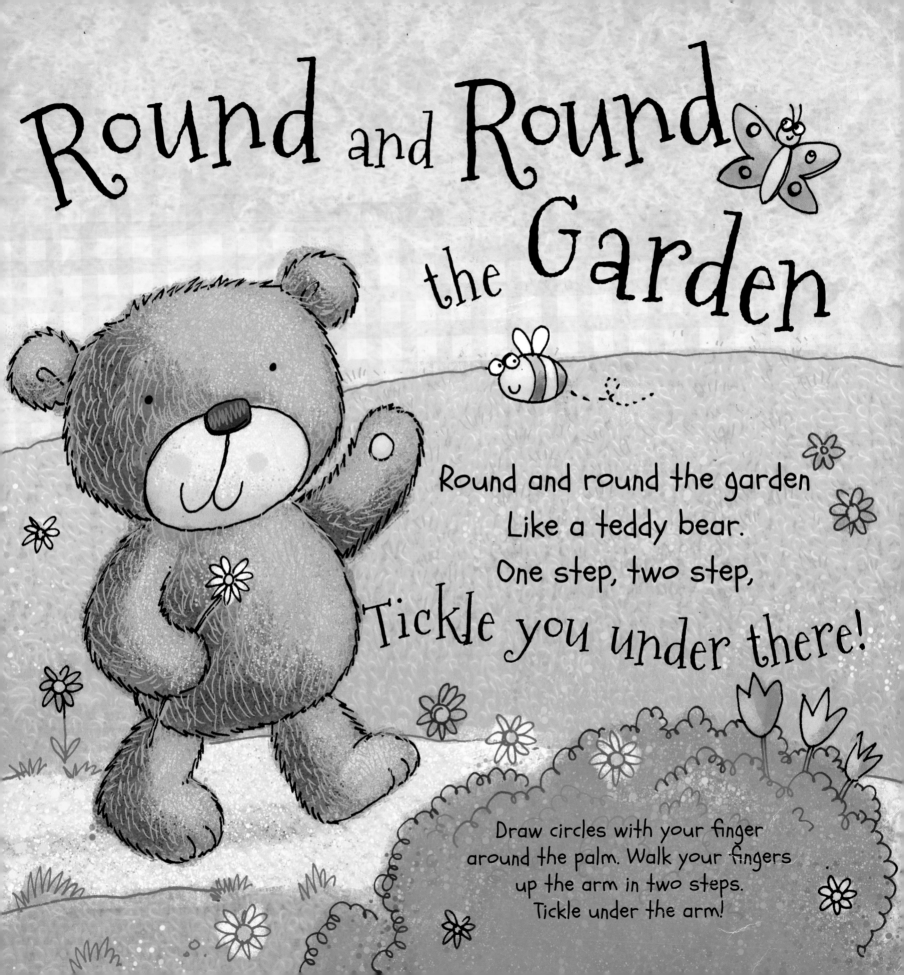

Round and Round the Garden

Round and round the garden
Like a teddy bear.
One step, two step,
Tickle you under there!

Draw circles with your finger
around the palm. Walk your fingers
up the arm in two steps.
Tickle under the arm!

Row, Row, Row Your Boat

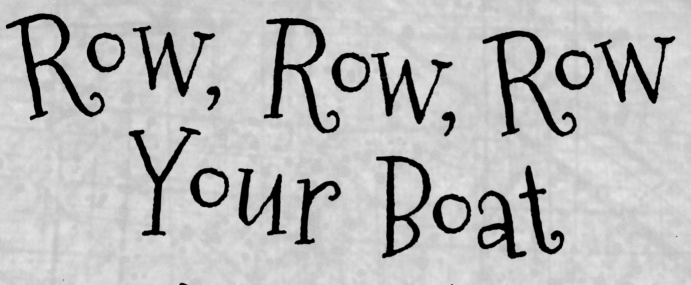

Row, row, row your boat
Gently down the stream.
Merrily, merrily, merrily, merrily,

Life is but a dream.

Sit across from your partner,
holding hands and rocking back and
forth. SCREAM on the second verse!
ROAR on the third verse!

Row, row, row your boat
Gently down the stream.
If you see a crocodile,
Don't forget to SCREAM!

Row, row, row your boat
Gently to the shore.
If you see a lion,
Don't forget to ROAR!

This Little Pig

Market

This little pig went to market,
This little pig stayed at home,
This little pig had roast beef,
This little pig had none,
And this little pig cried,
"Wee-Wee-Wee-Wee-wee!"
All the way home.

Pat-a-Cake

Pat-a-cake, pat-a-cake, baker's man,

Bake me a cake as fast as you can.

Roll it and pat it and mark it with 'B',

And put it in the oven for

baby and me.

Clap your hands together then
pat the palms of your partner.
Repeat this action as you sing the rhyme.

I'm a Little Teapot

Place one hand on your hip to be the handle. Place the other arm out to the side to be the spout. On the final line, lean over to one side to pour the tea.

I'm a little teapot
Short and Stout,
Here is my handle
Here is my spout.

When I see the teacups
Hear me shout,
"Tip me up and pour me out!"

If You're Happy and you Know it

If you're happy and you know it,

Clap your hands!

If you're happy and you know it,

Clap your hands!

Repeat the words again, but change the action to stamping your feet, clicking your fingers and nodding your head.

If you're happy and you know it
And you really want to show it,
If you're happy and you know it
Clap your hands!

The Grand Old Duke of York

Oh, the grand old Duke of York,
He had ten thousand men,
He marched them up to the top of the hill
And he marched them down again.

March up and down on the
spot to get to the top of the hill.
March and crouch down to get down hill.
March half-crouching half-standing
to be neither up nor down.

And when they were up they were up,
And when they were down they were down,
And when they were only halfway up,
They were neither up nor down.

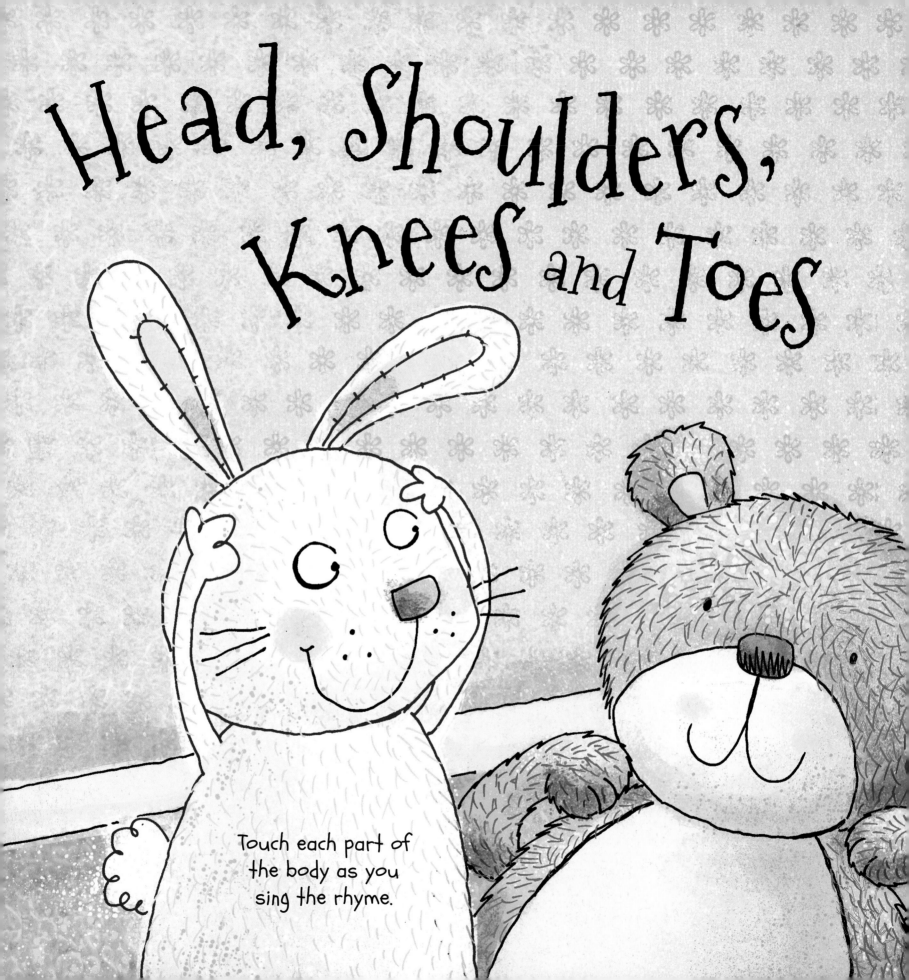

Head, Shoulders, Knees and Toes

Touch each part of the body as you sing the rhyme.

Head, shoulders, knees and toes,
Knees and toes.

Head, shoulders, knees and toes,
Knees and toes.

And eyes and ears and mouth and nose,

Head, shoulders, knees and toes,
Knees and toes.

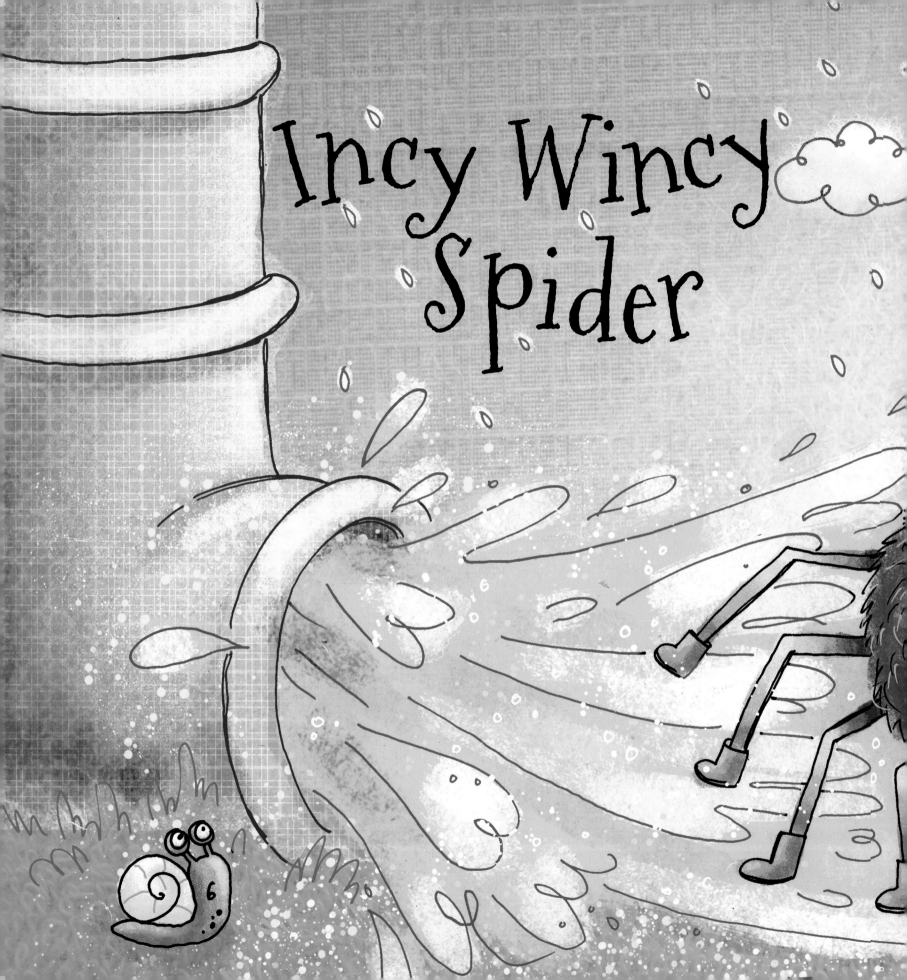

Incy Wincy Spider

See-saw, Margery Daw

See-saw, Margery Daw,

Johnny shall have a new master,

He shall have but a penny a day

Because he can't work any faster.

Sit on the floor facing your partner holding hands. Gently rock backwards and forwards as if you were on a see-saw.

I Hear Thunder

I hear thunder, I hear thunder,
Hark, don't you, hark, don't you?

Pitter patter raindrops,
Pitter patter raindrops,
I'm wet through,
So are you.

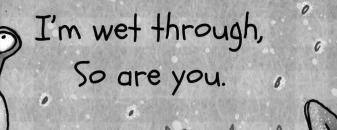

Stamp your feet on the ground to make thunder.
Wiggle your fingers to make raindrops.
Point to yourself. Point to your partner.

Ring-a-ring o' Roses

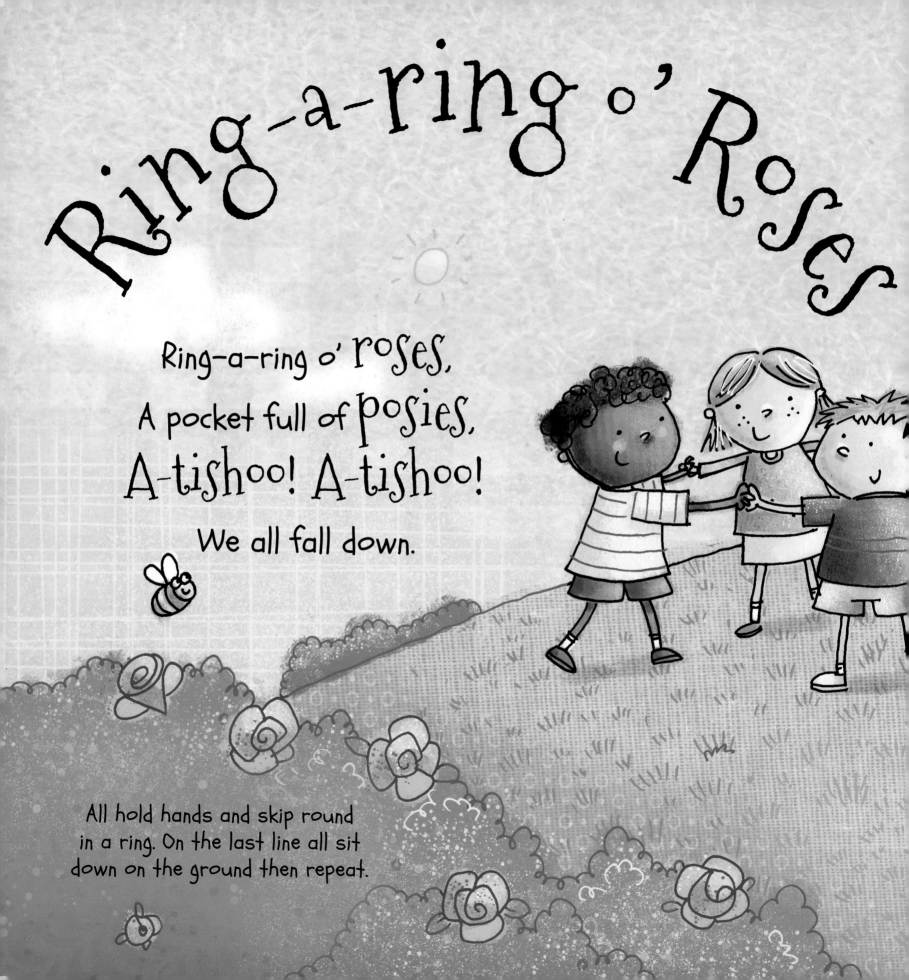

Ring-a-ring o' roses,
A pocket full of posies,
A-tishoo! A-tishoo!
We all fall down.

All hold hands and skip round
in a ring. On the last line all sit
down on the ground then repeat.

The king has sent his daughter
To fetch a pail of water,
A-tishoo! A-tishoo!
We all fall down.

The bird upon the steeple
Sits high above the people,
A-tishoo! A-tishoo!
We all fall down.

Rain

Rain on the green grass,
Rain on the trees,
Rain on the rooftop,
But not on me!

Make rain motions with your fingers. Sweep hands around to form a treetop. Form a roof over your head with your hands. Point to yourself with your index finger.

The End